FOCUS

POWERED BY

Practice Tests Plus

EXAM PRACTICE

CAMBRIDGE ENGLISH **PRELIMINARY**

Pearson Education Limited
Edinburgh Gate
Harlow
Essex CM20 2JE
and Associated Companies throughout the world.

www.pearsonelt.com/exams

The right of Russel Whitehead to be identified as author of this Work has been
asserted by him in accordance with the Copyright, Designs and Patents Act 1988.

First published 2016
Second impression 2016

ISBN: 978-1-292-12114-7
(Parts of Test 1 and Test 2 taken from Practice Tests Plus Cambridge English Preliminary 3)

Set in Arial
Printed in Slovakia by Neografia

Photo acknowledgements
The publisher would like to thank the following for their kind permission to reproduce
their photographs:

(Key: b-bottom; c-centre; l-left; r-right; t-top)

Alamy Images: Image Scotland 51, Imageshop 32tc, LOOK Die Bildagentur der
Fotografen GmbH 14, Brad Rickerby 32t, UpperCut Images 54; **Corbis:** Sandra Eckhardt
32b, Westend61 / Tom Chance 32bc; **Fotolia.com:** Jeffrey Banke 10c, erikdegraaf 36,
Kurhan 38, Martinan 10tc, Monkey Business 16, Photo_Ma 10bc, Westa Zikas 10t;
Getty Images: monkeybusinessimages 32c, Soul 10b; **Pearson Education Ltd:** 55;
Reuters: Jean-Paul Pelissier 53; **Thinkstock:** James Woodson 50

All other images © Pearson Education

Contents

Exam Overview

The **Cambridge English: Preliminary** exam, also known as the **Preliminary English Test (PET)** is an examination set at the B1 level of the Common European Framework of Reference for Languages (CEFR). It is made up of three papers, each testing a different area of ability in English: Reading and Writing, Listening and Speaking. Each of the four skills carries 25% of the marks.

Reading and Writing   1 hour 30 minutes

Listening   36 minutes (including 6 minutes to copy answers onto the answer sheet)

Speaking   10–12 minutes (for each pair of students)

All the examination questions are task-based. Rubrics (instructions) are important and should be read carefully. They set the context and give important information about the tasks. There are separate answer sheets for recording answers for the Reading and Writing and Listening papers.

Paper	Format	Task focus
Reading and Writing: Reading 5 tasks, 35 questions	**Part 1:** multiple choice Reading five short texts and answering five multiple-choice questions.	Reading short texts for the main message.
	Part 2: matching Matching five descriptions of people to eight short texts.	Reading for specific information and detailed comprehension.
	Part 3: true/false Reading a longer factual text and deciding if each of the ten statements is true or false.	Processing a factual text and scanning for specific information.
	Part 4: multiple choice Reading a longer text and answering five four-option multiple-choice questions.	Reading for detailed comprehension; understanding attitude, opinion and writer purpose.
	Part 5: multiple-choice cloze Choosing which word from a choice of four fits in each of ten gaps in the text.	Understanding vocabulary and grammar in a text.

Paper	Format	Task focus
Reading and Writing: Writing 3 parts, 7 questions	**Part 1:** sentence transformations Completing a second sentence so that it has the same meaning as the first sentence using no more than three words.	Knowledge of vocabulary and understanding of grammatical sentence structure.
	Part 2: communicative message Following instructions to write a short message of 35–45 words.	Communicating three specific points in writing.
	Part 3: continuous writing Producing one piece of writing of about 100 words, from a choice between an informal letter and a story.	Control and range of language in continuous text.
Listening 4 tasks, 25 questions	**Part 1:** multiple choice Listening to seven short monologues or dialogues and choosing the correct picture from a choice of three for each question.	Listening to identify key information.
	Part 2: multiple choice Listening to a longer monologue or interview and choosing the correct answer for six three-option multiple-choice questions.	Listening to identify specific information and detailed meaning.
	Part 3: gap-fill Listening to a longer monologue and completing the missing information in six gaps.	Listening to identify, understand and interpret information.
	Part 4: true/false Listening to an informal dialogue and deciding whether six statements are true or false.	Listening for detailed meaning and identifying the attitudes and opinions of the speakers.
Speaking 4 tasks	**Part 1:** examiner-led conversation	Giving personal information.
	Part 2: two-way collaborative task with visual prompts	Making and responding to suggestions, discussing alternatives, making recommendations and negotiating agreement.
	Part 3: individual long turn with visual prompt	Describing photographs using appropriate vocabulary and organising an extended turn.
	Part 4: two-way discussion	Talking about opinions, preferences, habits, etc.

Practice Test 1 with Guidance

Reading: Parts 1–5

About the paper

The *Reading and Writing* paper lasts for 1 hour and 30 minutes. It contains eight parts: five reading parts and three writing parts.

The Reading section includes a range of text types, for example, signs and notices, emails, extracts from magazine articles, texts, websites and brochures, and question types. This part of the paper tests your knowledge of vocabulary and grammar as well as your ability to read and understand a range of texts. There are 35 questions in total and each question is worth one mark.

In the Writing section, you will write a variety of text types from sentences to longer continuous writing. The first part tests your grammar and each question is worth one mark. The second and third parts test extended writing and are worth five marks and fifteen marks respectively.

Part 1: Multiple choice
In Part 1, you read five short information-based texts, for example signs, notices, emails, etc. For each question, you have to choose the best answer from a choice of three options.

Part 2: Matching
In Part 2, you read five short descriptions of people and eight short texts on the same topic, for example information about books or museums. You have to match each person to one of the texts.

Part 3: True/False
In Part 3, there is one long factual text and ten questions. You have to decide whether each question is true or false. The questions follow the order of the text.

Part 4: Multiple choice
In Part 4, there is one long text which includes attitude or opinion as well as facts. You have to answer five multiple-choice questions, each with four options. The questions follow the order of the text.

Part 5: Multiple-choice cloze
In Part 5, you read a short text and complete a multiple-choice cloze task. Ten words have been removed from the text. For each gap, you have to choose from four options the word which fits best.

How to do the paper

Part 1
- Read the instructions and look at the example.
- Read the first text and think about where you might see it and why it was written. Try to think of another way to say the same thing.
- Carefully read the three options (A, B and C) and decide which one has the same main meaning.
- If you are not sure which answer is correct, cross out any options that are clearly wrong, and then see which are left. If you're still not sure, you should guess. You do not lose marks for wrong answers and your guess may be right!

Part 2
- First read the instructions and the title above the short texts to get an idea of the topic.
- Read through the five descriptions of people and underline the key words.
- Quickly read each section of the main text and highlight information that matches the descriptions. Don't just look for the same words as they may not say the same thing. Look for different words or phrases that have the same meaning.
- Read each description again and carefully check the parts you highlighted in the texts to find the best match. The ideas in each description are likely to occur in more than one text, but only one text includes *all* of the things the person needs or wants.

Part 3
- In Part 3, you don't need to read the whole text first. The text contains some information that you won't need in order to answer the questions and will probably include vocabulary you don't know. But don't worry, you don't need to understand every word to be able to answer the questions.
- First read the instructions and the title of the text to get an idea of the topic.
- Read through all of the sentences and underline the key words.
- Quickly scan the text and highlight places where the information is talked about. Look for words and phrases that mean the same as the key words you underlined in the sentences.

- Remember that the sentences are always in the same order as the information in the text.
- Read the highlighted section of the text carefully and decide whether the sentence is true or false.

Part 4
- First read the instructions and the title of the text to get an idea of the topic.
- Read the text quickly to get a general understanding of what it's about and how it is organised.
- Read through the questions without looking at the options (A–D) and underline key words.
- The questions follow the order of the text. Find the section of text where a question is answered and read it carefully, underlining key words and phrases.
- Try to answer the question without looking at the four answer options. Then read the options and choose the one that is closest to your own answer. Look for the same meaning expressed in a different way.
- Check that the other options are all clearly wrong. If you are still unsure, read the text again very carefully and look for reasons why some of the options may be wrong.
- For questions 21 and 25, you have to think about the whole of the text. Try to answer without looking at the options and then choose the best answer.

Part 5
- Read the text quickly, ignoring the gaps, to get a general understanding.
- Read the text again. At each space, stop and try to work out what the missing word might be.
- Look at the options (A–D) and decide which one fits the gap. Check the words before and after the gap, for example some words can only be followed by a certain preposition. Look at the whole sentence to check the meaning of the missing word.
- If you are not sure which word to choose, decide which options are clearly wrong and then see which are left. If you're still not sure, you should guess. You do not lose marks for wrong answers and your guess may be right.
- When you have finished, read the whole text again and check that it makes sense.

Questions 1–5

Look at the text in each question. What does it say?
Choose the correct letter **A**, **B** or **C**.
In the exam, you mark your answers **on a separate answer sheet**.

Example:

0

> Charlie,
> Please can you pick up my coat from the dry
> cleaner's when you collect your suit? I'll pay
> you back this afternoon, if that's OK.
> Thanks a lot!
> Vera

What will Charlie do?

A Receive the money for the dry cleaning later today.

B Take his clothes to the dry cleaner's.

C Fetch Vera's suit from the dry cleaner's.

0	A	B	C
	▬	▭	▭

1

> ## RIVER SCHOOL LIBRARY
> ___
> Wait in this area while
> your books are checked.
> Thank you.

A You must tell us if you leave books here for checking.

B Check that you have all your books before leaving the library.

C Do not leave here until we have checked your books.

2

> Countryside here's
> OK. Mountains higher
> than we expected. Very
> little wildlife, though
> the other people in the
> group are fun and we
> have easy transport.
> Deshini

In Deshini's opinion, what is the disadvantage of the place she is visiting?

A The transport.

B The animals.

C The mountains.

3

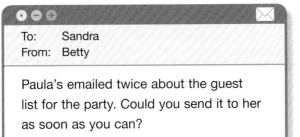

To: Sandra
From: Betty

Paula's emailed twice about the guest list for the party. Could you send it to her as soon as you can?

What does Sandra need to do?

A   Let Paula know who's going to the party.

B   Send a party invitation to Paula.

C   Ask Paula who should be invited to the party.

4

SOUTHWOOD COLLEGE CANTEEN

Staff and students cannot use the canteen without ID cards.

A   Students can get their ID cards in the canteen.

B   Staff must bring their ID cards if they want to eat at the canteen.

C   Students need to show staff their ID cards.

5

The football coach rang. Nobody from our team has booked to come at 2, only other teams. So this week we'll have to train at 4 instead.

A   We need to change the training time because it's full at 2 p.m. this week.

B   We may have to train with a different team this week.

C   We must go training at a later time this week.

Tip strip

Question 1: Is this a sign, a note or a label? <u>Underline</u> the words in A, B or C which have the same meaning as 'while your books are checked'.

Question 2: Which word or words in the notice have a negative effect? Does the word 'disadvantage' in the question relate to positive or negative things?

Question 3: How do you think Sandra, Betty and Paula are connected to each other? What does 'it' refer to in the question: 'Could you send *it* to her as soon as you can?'

Question 4: Where might you see this text? Does the text say that you can get an ID card in the canteen? Does the text talk about both staff and students?

Question 5: When is the training usually? What time are they going to train 'this week'?

Questions 6–10

The people below are all looking for a magazine to buy.
On the opposite page, there are eight advertisements for magazines.
Decide which magazine would be the most suitable for the following people.
For questions **6–10**, choose the correct letter (**A–H**). In the exam, you mark your answers **on a separate answer sheet**.

6

Omar is interested in architecture and wants to know more about it. He would like to meet people with the same interest and to visit special buildings locally.

7

Cecile is very keen on sport and keeping fit and particularly enjoys long-distance running. She would like to improve her technique and perhaps find other people to run with.

8

Duncan enjoys spending his free time in the countryside, exploring different areas on foot and by bike. He wants to know more about what he sees when he is exploring.

9

Heidi likes going to watch her favourite football team, although she usually has to work at weekends, organising jazz concerts and festivals. She's keen to learn about the history of football.

10

Piotr is studying IT and Business at university, but he's very interested in modern art, although he's usually too busy to visit galleries and museums.

Tip strip

Question 6: What three things does Omar want? Find a match for topic, people and location.

Question 7: What is Cecile's favourite thing to do? What does she want to do better? Where might she meet other people?

Question 8: What activities does Duncan like doing? Make sure you match both!

Question 9: How can Heidi find all the news if she can't attend a match?

Question 10: What is Piotr's interest? How much time does he have for his hobby?

This Month's Pick of the Magazines

A World of Sport

This is *the* magazine for sports fans! All team sports are covered. Missed a game? Don't worry – full reports on all games, as well as interviews with players and much more. There are lots of photos and special articles on subjects such as the early beginnings of football and baseball clubs in distant places.

B History is Beautiful

Art and music lovers will really enjoy this magazine. It's full of interesting articles about the history of concert music and classical architecture around the world and the development of the great museums and galleries.

C Footloose

Are you someone who loves being outside and looking after your body? *Footloose* is the magazine for the outdoor runner who takes their hobby seriously. Professional advice is given, with tips for achieving the best style on long runs. There are also lists of local clubs you can contact or join.

D Green World

The busier our city lives become, the more we want to escape to the fields and hills. *Green World* is the magazine to take with you. There's lots of information about birds, animals, trees and plants, together with maps of great bike rides and walks.

E Sport Business

Interested in sport? Want a career in sport? Want to study sport? This is the magazine for you! Maybe you want to learn about setting up a health club or a bike shop, or about how football clubs operate in the business world. It's all here!

F Plan for Success

This magazine is all about setting up businesses that will succeed in today's difficult economic climate. With articles by famous sportspeople and tips on how to run a company efficiently, you can learn all you need to get ahead.

G How We Live

Houses, offices, museums, bridges ... somebody designed them, somebody built them – but most people walk straight past them. Learn about the structures we live and work in. *How We Live* also contains a list of local groups, so you can share your enthusiasm with other people in your area.

H Pictures in Your Living Room

This is the magazine for today's art lover. Every month there are large high-quality reproductions of famous pictures from the 20th and 21st centuries. Whether you live in a student room or a castle, turn your home into an exhibition hall with these masterworks.

Questions 11–20

Look at the sentences below about two old ships in the UK.
Read the text on the opposite page to decide if each sentence is correct or incorrect.
If it is correct, write **A**.
If it is not correct, write **B**.
In the exam, you mark your answers **on a separate answer sheet**.

---

11 French ships came to England because of the English occupation of a part of France.

12 Henry VIII decided to control the battle at Portsmouth himself.

13 Nowadays, everybody knows the reason the *Mary Rose* sank.

14 Henry VIII wanted to rescue the *Mary Rose* after it sank.

15 The Mary Rose Museum opened in 1982.

16 The *Golden Hinde* was one of the ships Francis Drake took all the way around the world.

17 Drake returned to England with a lot of money.

18 Queen Elizabeth wanted people to visit the *Golden Hinde*.

19 The ship you can see today is the original *Golden Hinde*.

20 On the *Golden Hinde*, you can learn about how sailors found their way across the sea.

Tip strip

Question 11: Look for a reason for the French ships coming to England. What does 'In response' in line 4 refer to?

Question 12: Look for a phrase in the text that means the same as 'control' in the question.

Question 13: Does everyone agree on the reason that the ship sank?

Question 14: What did Henry try to do after the *Mary Rose* sank?

Question 15: Was the work on the *Mary Rose* completed in the year 1982?

Question 17: The text says that Drake 'became rich'. How did he do this?

Question 18: Why was the *Golden Hinde* important to Queen Elizabeth? How did she show this?

Question 19: Does 'a fully working model' mean the same as 'the original'?

Ships of History

If you're interested in history or ships, or both, there are two ships you must try to see in the UK — the *Mary Rose* and the *Golden Hinde*.

In 1543, Henry VIII went to war with France (not for the first time), and the next year he took control of the French town of Boulogne. In response, a large number of French ships set sail for England. The French had over 200 ships in their fleet and the English about 80, waiting near the town of Portsmouth on the South Coast. The leading ship was the *Mary Rose*, the biggest and best ship in England at that time. Henry VIII, although getting old and ill, arrived to take charge of the battle himself.

The French ships couldn't get into Portsmouth, because it was defended by towers and a castle, but they started firing at the English fleet. The English ships moved towards the French, but as the *Mary Rose* turned, it sank. There are several different theories as to why this happened, and one day we may know for sure.

Although Henry tried to have the *Mary Rose* brought up from the seabed, she remained underwater until 1982, when she was lifted out by the Mary Rose Trust. Careful work to repair and protect the ship began. After some years, this work was completed. Now visitors can view the special collection of thousands of personal, domestic and military objects in the Mary Rose Museum. With so much to see, you're sure to have an interesting time!

You could also come to London and see the *Golden Hinde*. This ship was famous as the flagship of Sir Francis Drake during his three-year voyage around the world, with the *Golden Hinde* being the only ship to return home safely, having left in 1577.

Drake captured many Spanish ships during the voyage, and took their gold and money. When Drake came back to England, he became both rich and famous. Queen Elizabeth I took a share of the prizes captured, and visited the *Golden Hinde* with great ceremony. She decided that the ship should be kept so that the general public could come and look at it, making it England's first museum ship.

The ship you can visit nowadays is a fully working model of the sixteenth-century ship, and has also sailed around the world. If history and sailing interest you, then attend a special workshop on the *Golden Hinde*. For the afternoon, you can become an officer on board and find out how to navigate the *Golden Hinde* in the way the original sailors did before modern electronic equipment was invented.

Questions 21–25

Read the text and questions below.
For each question, choose the correct letter **A**, **B**, **C** or **D**.
In the exam, you mark your answers **on a separate answer sheet**.

To Camp or Not to Camp?

When I asked a group of my friends this question, everybody had a strong opinion. Camping was either terrible or wonderful – there was nothing in between. I think it depends on your childhood: if you had fun camping when you were a kid, then that was the beginning of a life-long enjoyment. But the opposite could also be true! The message for families is clear.

Personally, I loved camping when I was a child and I still do today. My father worked in the oil industry and my family moved from city to city. I was quite lonely, I realise now. I never felt that the holidays we spent in other cities were real holidays; *real* holidays were the ones when we got out into the countryside and slept in tents. I think every family should have that experience. And even though I still live and work in a big city, this remains my opinion.

The camping I remember was out there, up mountains, in forests, by rivers – not stuck in campsites. If you're camping with friends or family, that's who you want to be with, not all the other people you meet in campsites. They're too safe – although they do have great showers and shops, and they are reasonable value for money. In fact, a night at a site once in a while lets you all get your clothes clean and stock up with food. But, wherever you go, don't pack lots of things: keep it basic and you'll have a better time.

We took my children camping last summer. We could see they loved it: the freedom, cooking on a fire, looking at the stars at night. I like to think that they understood the value of fresh air and water, sunshine, running and swimming, and that it meant more to them than expensive beach holidays.

Tip strip

Question 21: This question refers to the whole text. Look at **A**. Does the writer tell us how to prepare to go camping? Look at **B**. Does the writer say camping is a good thing to do and want other people to do it? Look at **C**. Does the text mainly contain detail about the writer's childhood holidays? Look at **D**. Does the writer think children should go camping without their parents?

Question 22: Does the writer say he spent a lot of time with his parents? What word suggests that he wasn't always happy? Was every holiday a camping holiday? What does he say about cities?

Question 23: Are there some examples of how a campsite can be useful? Are they expensive? Do they have the things you need or not? Does the writer mention making friends?

Question 24: See if you can find examples in the text of 'simple things', 'how to save money', 'names of stars' or 'how to cook food'.

Question 25: Look at the whole text again. Does the writer advise you to stay in campsites? Does he think all children enjoy camping? Does he think you need to take a lot of things when you go camping? Does he mention dangers?

21 What is the writer's main purpose in writing the text?

  A   To explain how to prepare for a camping trip.
  B   To encourage families to go camping together.
  C   To describe his childhood camping experiences.
  D   To persuade parents to let their children go camping.

22 What does the writer say in the second paragraph?

  A   He spent a lot of time with his parents when he was young.
  B   He had a happy childhood.
  C   He has always taken his holidays in the countryside.
  D   He has always lived in cities.

23 What does the writer say about campsites?

  A   It is useful to stay at campsites occasionally.
  B   It is too expensive to stay at campsites.
  C   They don't usually have enough facilities.
  D   They are a good place to make friends.

24 What does he hope his children learnt on their last camping holiday?

  A   The importance of simple things.
  B   How to save money.
  C   The names of stars.
  D   How to cook food.

25 What is the writer most likely to say?

  A   *If you go camping, take a map that shows where campsites are.*

  B   *People don't always realise that camping is enjoyed most by children.*

  C   *The less you take with you when camping, the more you'll enjoy it.*

  D   *Remember that camping can be quite dangerous, so plan your trip carefully.*

Tip strip

Question 26: There are two things, home and work. Which preposition is used to link two things like this?

Question 27: This is part of a set phrase.

Question 28: Which answer means 'similar to'?

Question 29: Which answer refers to the idea of the writer not knowing for sure?

Question 30: Which answer is closest in meaning to 'live'?

Question 31: This is part of a set phrase meaning 'an increasing number'.

Question 33: Only one word fits grammatically.

Question 34: Which word means the same as 'appropriate'?

Question 35: Which word means 'planned and made for a particular purpose'?

Questions 26–35

Read the text below and choose the correct word for each space.
For each question, choose the correct letter **A**, **B**, **C** or **D**.
In the exam, you mark your answers **on a separate answer sheet**.

Example:

| **0** | **A** For | **B** By | **C** From | **D** To |

0	A	B	C

Working from Home

(0) .... most people with jobs, some of the day is spent travelling **(26)** .... their home and their **(27)** .... of work. This can feel **(28)** .... a waste of time, but perhaps you can't afford to live near your office. Or you **(29)** .... want to have a big garden or **(30)** .... in the same neighbourhood as your family.

However, more and **(31)** .... people are changing their lives. They are working from home, **(32)** .... a room as their office, connected to their company by the internet. They **(33)** .... that this is a better way to work. They can work harder and they feel less tired.

If you want to do this, make sure you have a **(34)** .... room to work in, with a well **(35)** .... desk and chair. Of course, don't watch TV – and don't work for too long!

26	**A** among	**B** behind	**C** across	**D** between
27	**A** part	**B** position	**C** point	**D** place
28	**A** like	**B** so	**C** that	**D** as
29	**A** must	**B** may	**C** should	**D** can
30	**A** have	**B** become	**C** set	**D** be
31	**A** many	**B** much	**C** more	**D** most
32	**A** making	**B** doing	**C** using	**D** putting
33	**A** say	**B** inform	**C** tell	**D** speak
34	**A** correct	**B** suitable	**C** right	**D** successful
35	**A** designed	**B** invented	**C** discovered	**D** formed

Writing: Parts 1–3

About the paper

Part 1: Sentence transformations
In Part 1, you read five pairs of sentences which are all about the same topic and complete a sentence transformation task. The pairs of sentences have the same meaning, but are expressed in different ways. Between one and three words have been removed from the second sentence. You have to complete the second sentence using up to three words, so that it means the same as the first sentence.

Part 2: Communicative message
In Part 2, you have to write a short message, for example a note, an email or a postcard. You must include the three points given in the instructions. You should write between 35 and 45 words.

Part 3: Continuous writing
In Part 3, you must choose one question from a choice of two. You can choose to write an informal letter or a story. You should write around 100 words.

How to do the paper

Part 1
- Look at the instructions and the example to get an idea of the topic.
- Read the first sentence. Then read the second sentence and think about what is being tested, e.g. active to passive form.
- Decide what is missing from the second sentence and write the missing words.
- Your answer may include words or expressions not used in the first sentence, but these must express exactly the same idea. Do not include new information or change the information.
- Make sure you have not written more than three words. Remember that contracted words count as two words, e.g. *won't = will not*.
- Check that the sentences make sense and that you have spelled the words correctly.

Part 2
- Don't be in a hurry to start writing. It's worth spending a few minutes planning! Read the instructions carefully to understand:
  - who you are writing to and why.
  - what three pieces of information you have to include in your answer.
- Look again at the three written points and think about words and phrases you could use for each point. Think about what tense you will use for each one.
- Write between 35 and 45 words. Remember to start with a greeting (e.g. *Hi Anna*) and to add your name to sign off at the end.
- When you have finished, check your writing. Have you included all three points? Are there any basic mistakes that you can correct?

Part 3
- In Part 3, you can choose to write either a letter or a story. Don't be in hurry to start writing. Look carefully at each task and:
  - think about letter-writing: Are you confident you know how to write a letter to a friend? Do you know how to use the functional language you will need for this particular task (e.g. describing something, giving advice, etc.)?
  - think about writing a story: Look at the first line or title. Do you have an idea for a story? Can you think of some interesting language you can use?
- Part 3 gives you a chance to show the examiner the range of language and structures that you know. Choose the task where you are most confident.
- **Letter:** You are given part of a letter from an English-speaking friend and must write a reply. Read the instructions carefully and underline the things you must include in your letter. Remember to: start and end appropriately (e.g. *Hi Tom; All the best, Alex*), use informal language and be friendly throughout.
- **Story:** You are given either the title or the first line of the story. Make sure your story follows on from this, or you will lose marks. Be careful with names or pronouns in the title or first line and make sure your story continues with these. The story tests your ability to organise ideas into a beginning, middle and end, so pay attention to the structure of what you write and how you link ideas.
- For the task you choose, jot down the ideas that come into your head, in any order. Then choose your best ideas and decide how you will organise them into paragraphs.
- Write an answer using appropriate format and style.
- Write around 100 words.
- When you have finished, check your writing. Have you included everything from the instructions? Have you used varied language? Are your points clearly expressed?

Writing: Part 1

Questions 1–5

Tip strip

Question 1: Read the first sentence. What information does it give you about Machu Picchu? What kind of structure does it use? Now read the second sentence. How does it begin? How does it end? How can you complete it? Pay particular attention to the word 'as' after the gap.

Question 2: What is the subject of the verb 'hid'?

Question 5: How can we say 'if not' in a different way, in one word?

Here are some sentences about a place called Machu Picchu, in Peru.
For each question, complete the second sentence so that it means the same as the first.
Use no more than three words.
Write only the missing words.
In the exam, you write your answers **on a separate answer sheet**.
You may use this page for any rough work.

Example:

0 Nobody ever forgets seeing Machu Picchu.

Everybody always .... **Machu Picchu.**

| **0** | *remembers seeing* |

---

1 Machu Picchu is the most important historical site in South America.

Other historical sites in South America are not ....
as Machu Picchu.

2 Plants and trees hid the ancient city from people for hundreds of years.

The ancient city .... **from people by plants and trees for hundreds of years.**

3 The site contains the remains of many different buildings.

There .... **the remains of many different buildings at the site.**

4 The tourist train to the site doesn't travel very quickly.

The tourist train travels .... **to the site.**

5 If Machu Picchu isn't protected, tourists will damage it.

Tourists will damage Machu Picchu ....
is protected.

Writing: Part 2

Tip strip

Plan your answer before you start.

- Who are you going to write to?
- Why are you writing the note?
- What will you say first in your note? Think of an idea for what present Julie sent you.
- Why do you like the present? Which verb tense will you use in your answer to this point?
- What did you do on your birthday? Which verb tense will you use in your answer to this point?

When you finish, check your answer for simple mistakes. Make sure you have written about all three points.

Question 6

Your English friend, Julie, sent you a birthday present.

Write a note to send to Julie. In your note, you should:

- thank her for the present
- explain why you like it
- describe what you did on your birthday.

Write **35–45 words**. In the exam, you write your answer **on a separate answer sheet**.

Write an answer to **one** of the questions (**7** or **8**) in this part.
Write your answer in about **100 words**. In the exam, you write your answer **on a separate answer sheet**.

Question 7

• This is part of a letter you received from your English pen-friend.

> I really like going to the cinema. What kinds of film do you like? Tell me about them. Why do you like them?

• Now write a **letter** to your pen-friend about films.

Question 8

• Your English teacher has asked you to write a story.
• Your story must begin with this sentence:

I was glad when my phone started to ring.

• Now write your **story**.

Parts 1–4

About the paper

The *Listening* paper lasts for a little more than 30 minutes. It contains four parts with a total of 25 questions, each carrying one mark. It includes recordings of varying lengths and these could be monologues or dialogues. You will hear each recording twice. You have time to read the questions before you listen. This paper tests your ability to understand recorded texts and identify and interpret information.

Part 1: Multiple choice

In Part 1, you listen to seven short unrelated recordings. They may be monologues or dialogues. For each recording, you have to choose the correct answer from a choice of three pictures.

Part 2: Multiple choice

In Part 2, you listen to a longer monologue or an interview. You have to listen and answer six three-option multiple-choice questions.

Part 3: Gap-fill

In Part 3, you listen to a longer monologue. You are given a page of notes which summarise the content of the text. Six pieces of information are missing. You have to listen and complete the gaps, usually with a single word.

Part 4: True/False

In Part 4, you listen to a longer, informal dialogue. You listen and look at a list of six statements. You have to decide whether each statement is correct and answer 'Yes' or 'No'.

How to do the paper

Part 1
- Before you listen to each recording, look at the question and the pictures in order to prepare for what you are going to hear.
- The first time you listen, try to get a general understanding and choose the best option. Remember that there may be a reference to all of the options, but only one option answers the question.
- The second time you listen, check carefully to ensure that your answer is correct.

Part 2
- Before you listen, read the rubric (instructions) and the questions to give you a general understanding of what the recording will be about.
- Listen carefully for the detail. More than one of the options will be mentioned in the recording, but only one of them answers the question.
- Listen again to check that your answers are correct.

Part 3
- Before you listen, read the rubric, the title and the notes. Think about the type of information that is missing in each sentence. It may be a word or a number. Occasionally it will be two words.
- Listen and complete the gaps. If you miss a detail, don't worry. Carry on to the next gap and the next piece of information.
- When you listen a second time, complete any missing information and check your answers.

Part 4
- Before you listen, read the rubric and the six statements. Many of the questions are about whether the speakers agree or disagree, so be ready to listen out for this.
- As you listen, tick 'Yes' or 'No' for each statement. If you are not sure about one, don't worry. Move on to the next one.
- When you listen a second time, pay particular attention to any statements you were not sure about and check your answers.

Questions 1–7

There are seven questions in this part.
For each question there are three pictures and a short recording.
Choose the correct picture and put a tick (✓) in the box below it.

Example: Which are Sara's cousins?

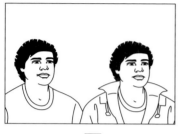

A ✓

B ☐

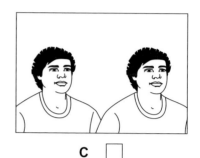

C ☐

---

1 What time does the film start?

A ☐

B ☐

C ☐

2 Which picture does the boy want?

A ☐

B ☐

C ☐

3 How does Valentina get from her house to school?

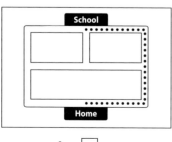

A ☐

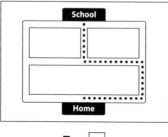

B ☐

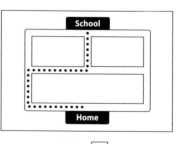

C ☐

4 What does Sally need?

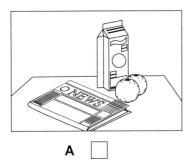 **A** ☐

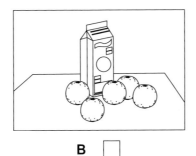 **B** ☐

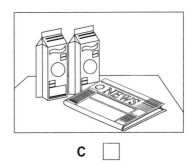 **C** ☐

5 What did the man forget to pack?

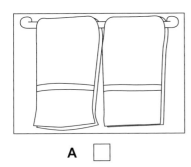 **A** ☐

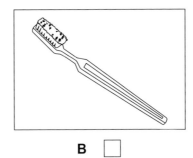 **B** ☐

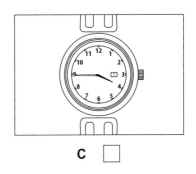 **C** ☐

6 What problem is there in the town?

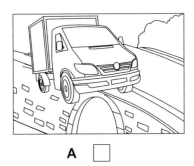 **A** ☐

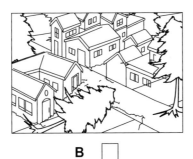 **B** ☐

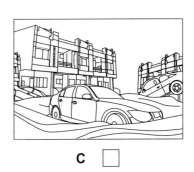 **C** ☐

7 What needs to be repaired?

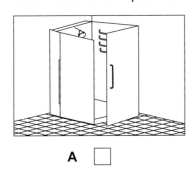 **A** ☐

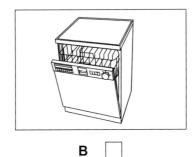 **B** ☐

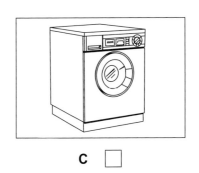 **C** ☐

Tip strip

Question 1: Pay attention to what the boy says. He says what time he is leaving, but he also gives the time of the film.

Question 3: What is the first thing that Valentina does when she comes out of her house?

Question 5: Why is the toothpaste 'useless'?

Question 7: What does the machine wash?

Tip strip

Question 8: Listen for the word 'mostly', a synonym of 'usually'. What number comes after it?

Question 10: What made walking easier for Ronald: the direction of the wind or the position of the sun?

Question 12: What does Ronald say is 'the best thing'?

Part 2

Questions 8–13

You will hear a radio interview with Ronald Ferguson, who has just walked across Scotland from coast to coast.
For each question, put a tick (✓) in the correct box.

8   How far did Ronald usually walk each day?

    A   about 11 miles ☐

    B   about 13 miles ☐

    C   about 18 miles ☐

9   How did Ronald prepare for the walk?

    A   He climbed several mountains. ☐

    B   He went walking every weekend. ☐

    C   He went to fitness classes. ☐

10 Ronald started in Oban because

    A   the wind made walking easier. ☐

    B   the sun was usually behind him. ☐

    C   the weather was better than in the east. ☐

11 Where did Ronald usually sleep?

    A   in guesthouses ☐

    B   beside the path ☐

    C   in a campsite ☐

12 What did Ronald enjoy most about the walk?

    A   the scenery ☐

    B   watching animals ☐

    C   being alone ☐

13 During the walk Ronald planned

    A   a book. ☐

    B   a holiday. ☐

    C   a talk. ☐

Tip strip

Question 14: Who will the trip be 'of particular interest' to?

Question 16: This is something that an activity will 'teach you about'.

Question 19: This information comes immediately after the number of nights.

Questions 14–19

You will hear a teacher talking to a group of schoolchildren about a school trip. For each question, fill in the missing information in the numbered space.

School Trip to Cardiff

Mainly for students of **(14)** _____

First day:

- Visit to Welsh Assembly

- Tour of the building

- Talk by government minister about the Assembly and improvements to **(15)** _____

Second day:

- Morning: tour of Cardiff Castle and chance to learn about **(16)** _____ in the Middle Ages

- Afternoon: talk by member of City Council about the protection of **(17)** _____

Practical information:

   Dates: 22–25 June

   Travel: by coach to Swindon and then by **(18)** _____

   Accommodation: in a **(19)** _____

Tip strip

Question 20: Max describes food he often eats. Is this a reason to eat the same thing again?

Question 22: This question asks about whether the speakers agree or not. You have to listen very carefully to both of them. Jenni expresses an opinion followed by 'but'. Listen to Max's response to her question.

Question 25: Max suggests they do this. What does Jenni remind him about?

Questions 20–25

Look at the six sentences for this part.
You will hear a girl, Jenni, and a boy, Max, planning dinner in a restaurant for their class.
Decide if each sentence is correct or incorrect.
If it is correct, put a tick (✓) in the box under **A** for **YES**. If it is not correct, put a tick (✓) in the box under **B** for **NO**.

		A YES	B NO
20	Max wants to have the food that he usually eats.	☐	☐
21	The Chinese restaurant will be closed.	☐	☐
22	They have both been to the Mexican restaurant.	☐	☐
23	Max wants to go to a restaurant with live music.	☐	☐
24	They agree to set a fixed price for the meal.	☐	☐
25	The whole class will choose the restaurant.	☐	☐

Parts 1–4

About the paper

The *Speaking* test lasts for 10–12 minutes. It contains four parts and carries 25% of the total mark. There are two candidates and two examiners. One examiner interacts with the candidates and the other examiner acts as the assessor and does not join in the conversation. The candidates are assessed on their performance of the whole test.

Part 1: Interview (2–3 minutes)
In Part 1, the examiner asks you and your partner questions in turn. These are questions about your personal details, daily routines, likes and dislikes, etc.

Part 2: Collaborative task (2–3 minutes)
In Part 2, you and your partner are given spoken instructions and a set of pictures as a basis for discussion and a task. You have to give your opinion as well as listen to and elicit the opinions of your partner, reaching an agreement if possible.

Part 3: Extended turn (3 minutes)
In Part 3, you and your partner are each given a colour photograph related to the same topic. You have to talk about your photograph for approximately one minute, describing it in as much detail as possible.

Part 4: Discussion (3 minutes)
In Part 4, the interlocutor sets up a task which is related to the topic of the photographs in Part 3. You have a conversation with your partner, giving your opinions on the topic, talking about personal experiences and your likes and dislikes as well as eliciting ideas from your partner.

How to do the paper

Part 1
- Listen carefully to the examiner's questions and to your partner's answers, as you might be asked the same or a similar question, or a completely different one.
- Give full answers, including relevant details.

Part 2
- Listen carefully to the instructions.
- Explore each of the suggestions in the pictures. Don't be afraid to give opinions and make comments, agreeing or disagreeing with your partner.
- When reaching a decision, remember there are no right or wrong choices and that you won't be given marks on your opinions but on the language you produce.

Part 3
- Describe the photograph in as much detail as possible, including the colour of clothing or objects, the weather and the time of day, for example. Try to imagine that you are describing it to someone who cannot see it.
- If you do not know or cannot remember the name of an object, describe what it looks like and what it is used for.

Part 4
- Listen carefully to the task.
- Cover the points in as much detail as you can and express your ideas clearly.
- Remember to involve your partner in the discussion, asking for his/her opinion and whether he/she agrees with you.

Tip strip

Part 1

- Practise spelling out your first name and surname so that you can do this easily.
- Be ready to talk about your study or work and what you do in your spare time. Prepare important vocabulary, but don't learn whole answers.
- Try to include as much detail as possible.

PART 1 (2–3 minutes)

Phase 1

Good morning/afternoon/evening. My name is … and this is … .

Now, what's your name, (*Candidate A*)?

Thank you.

And what's your name, (*Candidate B*)?

Thank you.

(*Candidate B*), what's your surname? How do you spell it?

And (*Candidate A*), what's your surname? How do you spell it?

Ask both candidates the following questions. Ask Candidate A first.

- Where do you live/come from?

Adult students

- Do you work or are you a student in …?
- What do you do/study?

School-age students

- Do you study English at school?
- Do you like it?

Thank you.

Phase 2

Select one or more questions from the list to ask each candidate. Ask Candidate B first.

- Do you enjoy studying English? Why?
- Do you think that English will be useful for you in the future?
- What did you do yesterday evening/last weekend?
- What do you enjoy doing in your free time?

Thank you.

Part 2
- You can ask and answer questions like: *Which activities will be most popular with the members? Do you think this one is a good idea? Do you think it's better to be indoors or outdoors?*
- Listen to your partner's opinions and agree or disagree. You could say: *I'm not sure about that idea.* or: *That sounds good.*

Part 3
- Start with where the people are and what they are doing.
- How do you think the people are feeling? Why do you think this?
- Give some other details about what you can see, for example, what people are wearing and what there is around them.

Part 4
- You could say: *People use computers for work and for entertainment.* Can you think of other examples?
- For your personal experience, you could say: *I use my computer to study English at school. Sometimes I play computer games with my friends.*
- Ask for your partner's opinions. Are they the same as yours or different?

PART 2 (2–3 minutes)

I'm going to describe a situation to you.

An English language club is planning to celebrate its tenth anniversary. Talk together about the different things they can do to celebrate the tenth anniversary, and then decide which one would be best.

Here is a picture with some ideas to help you. [*Turn to the picture on page 49.*]

I'll say that again.

An English language club is planning to celebrate its tenth anniversary. Talk together about the different things they can do to celebrate the tenth anniversary, and then decide which one would be best.

All right? Talk together.

PART 3 (3 minutes)

Now I'd like each of you to talk on your own about something. I'm going to give each of you a photograph of people using computers.

Candidate A, here is your photograph. [*Look at the photograph on page 50.*] Please show it to Candidate B, but I'd like you to talk about it. Candidate B, you just listen. I'll give you your photograph to talk about in a moment.

Candidate A, please tell us what you can see in the photograph.
(approximately 1 minute)

Thank you.

Now, Candidate B, here is your photograph. [*Look at the photograph on page 51.*] It also shows people using computers. Please show it to Candidate A and tell us what you can see in the photograph.
(approximately 1 minute)

Thank you.

PART 4 (3 minutes)

Your photographs showed people using computers. Now I'd like you to talk together about the things people use computers for and what you use a computer for.

Thank you. That is the end of the test.

Practice Test 2

Reading: Part 1

Questions 1–5

Look at the text in each question. What does it say?
Choose the correct letter **A**, **B** or **C**.
In the exam, you mark your answers **on a separate answer sheet**.

Example:

0

> Charlie,
> Please can you pick up my coat from the dry
> cleaner's when you collect your suit? I'll pay
> you back this afternoon, if that's OK.
> Thanks a lot!
> Vera

What will Charlie do?

A Receive the money for the dry cleaning later today.

B Take his clothes to the dry cleaner's.

C Fetch Vera's suit from the dry cleaner's.

1

> To: Carlos
> From: Lisa
>
> Good holiday? When you're back at
> college, don't forget to sign up for the
> language course. Tell me if you need
> some more information about it.

Why has Lisa contacted Carlos?

A To tell him about her holiday.

B To remind him to do something.

C To give him some details.

2

£30 TO RESERVE
any photograph
in the exhibition

A You must pay £30 if you want to display
photographs.

B We will keep a photograph for you if you pay £30.

C Some of the photos in the exhibition are reserved.

3

Elsa,

So nice to see you last night! I meant to ask you more about your new job. Brilliant! I'm sure you're pleased! Let's have lunch soon.

Shakeh

What is Shakeh doing in this card?

A Offering Elsa her congratulations.

B Providing some new information.

C Thanking Elsa for her lunch.

4

COLLEGE HOLIDAYS

After next Thursday,
the Study Centre will be closed
during evenings and weekends.

The Study Centre will

A open again for students on Friday.

B open for fewer hours until Thursday.

C change its opening hours from Thursday.

5

We're staying at the Regent Hotel. It's not the one we tried to book first, but it doesn't matter: this one's actually nearer the beach – where I'm spending all my time!

Keiko

What does Keiko feel about the Regent Hotel?

A She wishes it was closer to the beach.

B She prefers a different hotel.

C She thinks it has an advantage.

Reading: Part 2

Questions 6–10

The people below all want to watch a TV programme.
On the opposite page, there are descriptions of eight TV programmes.
Decide which programme would be most suitable for the following people.
For questions **6–10**, choose the correct letter (**A–H**). In the exam, you mark your answers
on a separate answer sheet.

6

Rita and Patsy are interested in dance. They like both modern and traditional ballet, and enjoy learning about the dancers' experiences and ideas. They often go out in the evening.

7

Charlie and Petra are very keen on nature, particularly wildlife and the Antarctic. They enjoy experts discussing environmental issues, but they don't like phone-in programmes.

8

Roger and Martin both go cycling every weekend, entering short- and long-distance races. They want to be as fit as possible and also learn about the history of cycle racing.

9

Penny and Paul enjoy live arts, especially theatre and classical music concerts. They live in the countryside and cannot go to the city very often.

10

Danni and Fred are interested in exploration, especially people who go on trips for the first time or in unusual ways. They would like to plan a trip themselves one day.

TV Programmes

A Stage Sensational

Three young actors play in this new evening series about a drama club. Keen to escape from the traditional approach of the school, they develop their own modern style – but can they manage to show it in public performances?

B One Man and His Bike

The longest journey: whether this is your first viewing or you are returning to keep up-to-date, you'll be entertained by Harry Lomas' self-recorded commentary. Harry describes his strange experiences as he rides around the world on his old red bike, following routes nobody's tried before. Tonight he meets a bear.

C Animal Access

If you're concerned about green issues and if you care about wild animals, here's the programme for you. Join our panel discussion by phoning in with your questions or suggestions for keeping our planet safe for animals, and you could even win the top prize: a trip to Antarctica.

D Moving Story

Follow the joys and heartaches of a junior dance school's attempts to reach the national final championships in different styles. Every afternoon, you can see an update of their progress, and you can phone in to vote on individual performances.

E The Road to Success

An enjoyable biography of one of the fastest cyclists of all time. Mixing old sections of film with current interviews – and even the chance to phone in with your own questions about technique and so on – this programme will inspire you to ride faster yourself.

F The Last Paradise

The white frozen landscape of the South Pole is said to be the last place man hasn't damaged beyond repair. Watch the fascinating filming of native animals and birds. You'll feel as if you're there yourself with some of the creative new camera techniques.

G Perfect Performances

Whether your tastes are traditional or more modern, you'll love this celebration of plays and operas, each one performed to the highest standards and broadcast to your living room. Additional information about history and background is available interactively.

H Routes and Riding

This programme is for both children and parents, and is designed to get children riding bikes and exploring the countryside. It encourages them to get fitter and healthier and learn more about the natural world around them. Special routes are shown for first-time riders.

Reading: Part 3

Questions 11–20

Look at the sentences below about cycling holidays.
Read the text on the opposite page to decide if each sentence is correct or incorrect.
If it is correct, write **A**.
If it is not correct, write **B**.
In the exam, you mark your answers **on a separate answer sheet**.

---

11 You will get advice about how to cycle correctly.

12 Food is provided for free during the day.

13 You do not have to carry your own bags on your bicycle.

14 The distance you cycle changes according to how hilly or flat the roads are each day.

15 You can go on a tour of a lake in a boat.

16 Guests will stay in hotels of a different standard each night.

17 It costs more if you want to stay in a single room.

18 You can choose what kind of meal you want to eat in the evening.

19 The largest tour group is fifteen guests.

20 Children under fourteen can come on these holidays with their parents.

Blue Sky Cycling Holidays

Wondering where to go for your holidays this year? Tired of beach holidays? Looking for a holiday with a bit more zing? Are you ready to try something new? If your answer is 'yes' to these questions, then the solution is obvious: join us on a Blue Sky Cycling Holiday!

Get fit while you relax on holiday. Each cycling group is joined by two expert guides and tour leaders. As well as being great fun, they are qualified fitness trainers, so they will make sure you cycle in the right way. What you eat is, of course, up to you! We will be passing through villages with very special local foods for your lunch, so you can buy what you prefer.

And don't worry about trying to carry all your luggage on your bike. This will be taken from hotel to hotel in our cars, ready for you when you arrive each evening. The distance we cover each day will depend on the kind of countryside we're travelling through, so you'll never get too tired. Our routes are carefully planned to include many places of interest, with frequent breaks to enjoy a coffee, a tour of an old castle or a rest by the side of a lake.

Accommodation is arranged for you in good-quality 3-star hotels. Experience has taught us that this is the standard most people prefer on our holidays.

Our prices are per person, based on sharing a twin room, but single accommodation is available for a small extra payment at the time of booking. There is a choice of breakfasts, from tea and fruit to complete cooked breakfasts, and, similarly, in the evenings, you can help yourself from a buffet or go for the set menu.

In order to keep the groups friendly and safe on the roads, we set a limit on the number of people on a holiday. This varies to some extent depending on the landscape and road types being used on any particular holiday, but we don't run holidays with fewer than six guests or more than fifteen. In addition to this, we set a limit of no more than five children in any group, and they must be accompanied by at least one parent. We also hope you will understand that these holidays aren't suitable for children under the age of fourteen.

Call or email for more information or to make a booking today!

Questions 21–25

Read the text and questions below.
For each question, choose the correct letter **A**, **B**, **C** or **D**.
In the exam, you mark your answers **on a separate answer sheet**.

By Design

Years ago, when I first thought of becoming a designer, people just didn't seem to be very interested in design. These days, however, there always seems to be some series on TV about design and there are all sorts of qualifications you can get. Nowadays, a lot of IT designers seem to think they are the most important designers, that their work is more interesting than anyone else's. The reality is that we've had designers throughout our history. They have made pyramids, scientific instruments, things to sit on, clothes to wear … What would life be like without them?

Boats can be quite a good way of understanding this point. Sea transport was crucial for the development of our civilization – we spread our population, we got new kinds of food and raw materials. It's amazing to think how far people explored in ancient boats. Modern boats are packed with sophisticated computer equipment to help sailors find their way, avoid storms and so on, yet we discovered new lands without all that. Pay attention to those old boats: they float, they move in the right direction, and they are pleasing to look at. We want things to look good and work well.

Food raises the same issues. Many of us use tools rather than our hands to prepare and eat food, finding new ways to make the process easier. In the West, people use knives and forks; in the East, they use chopsticks – these tools are unlike each other in appearance, but they do a similar job. Throughout history, great value has always been placed on the appearance of these tools. This is why we depend on design, linking our past and present and one country with another.

21 What is the writer's main purpose in writing the text?

    A To encourage people to try to become designers.

    B To list the different stages in the history of design.

    C To explain why most people do not like design.

    D To show the general importance of design in the world.

22 What do we learn about the writer from the text?

    A He thinks some designers are too self-centred.

    B He trained as a designer.

    C He thinks there should be more designers.

    D He wants to make TV programmes about design.

23 What point is made about boats?

    A Ancient boats were very sophisticated.

    B Boat design mixes practical and visual aspects.

    C Modern boats are not beautiful to look at.

    D Few boats are used for exploring.

24 The writer says that tools for eating

    A have changed very little over time.

    B are often not very easy to use.

    C are different in different cultures.

    D have become more important socially in recent years.

25 What might the writer of this article say?

    A *Transport and food have always been regarded as the two most important types of design.*

    B *It's disappointing to realise that a large number of designers are not professionally qualified.*

    C *It's exciting to think of the effect computers are going to have on design in the future.*

    D *There are several different things to think about when you look at how something is designed.*

Questions 26–35

Read the text below and choose the correct word for each space.
For each question, choose the correct letter **A**, **B**, **C** or **D**.
In the exam, you mark your answers **on a separate answer sheet**.

Example:

0   **A**   seems   **B**   reviews   **C**   looks   **D**   supposes

0	A	B	C	D
	▬	▭	▭	▭

In Tune

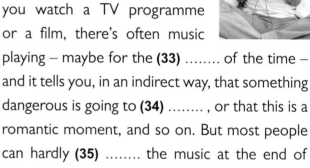

It **(0)** .... that music is almost as old as human life itself. If we knock two objects **(26)** .... at regular intervals, for example, the **(27)** .... is a rhythm, or a kind of music. It has a meaning **(28)** .... us.

Music has the power to change how we feel. It can **(29)** .... us excited – but it can also **(30)** .... a feeling of sadness. In our minds, we connect certain pieces of music with particular people or places.

However, sometimes we almost **(31)** .... to realise the effect of music. For example, **(32)** .... you watch a TV programme or a film, there's often music playing – maybe for the **(33)** .... of the time – and it tells you, in an indirect way, that something dangerous is going to **(34)** .... , or that this is a romantic moment, and so on. But most people can hardly **(35)** .... the music at the end of the programme.

26 A ahead	**B** together	**C** alike	**D** next
27 A result	**B** end	**C** final	**D** answer
28 A at	**B** on	**C** for	**D** by
29 A make	**B** do	**C** put	**D** go
30 A design	**B** invent	**C** discover	**D** create
31 A lose	**B** fall	**C** miss	**D** fail
32 A when	**B** how	**C** then	**D** where
33 A most	**B** majority	**C** matter	**D** maximum
34 A set	**B** take	**C** happen	**D** become
35 A fasten	**B** remind	**C** forget	**D** remember

Writing: Part 1

Questions 1–5

Here are some sentences about moving house.
For each question, complete the second sentence so that it means the same as the first.
Use no more than three words.
Write only the missing words.
In the exam, you write your answers **on a separate answer sheet**.
You may use this page for any rough work.

Example:

0   Ian moved to his new house two weeks ago.

Ian's lived in his new house .... **two weeks.**

0	for

---

1   His new house is taller than the other houses in the street.

His new house is .... **house in the street.**

2   His old friend Fred lives in the same street.

Fred, an old friend .... **lives in the same street.**

3   There's a beautiful view from Ian's balcony.

Ian's balcony .... **a beautiful view.**

4   He had quite a small house before.

He .... **to have quite a small house.**

5   He was given help moving by his family.

His family .... **help with moving.**

Writing: Part 2

Question 6

You want to spend Saturday with your friend.

Write an email to your friend. In your email, you should:

- ask if your friend is free
- explain what you want to do together
- suggest where to meet.

Write **35–45 words**. In the exam, you write your answer **on a separate answer sheet**.

Writing: Part 3

Write an answer to **one** of the questions (**7** or **8**) in this part.
Write your answer in about **100 words**. In the exam, you write your answer **on a separate answer sheet**.

Question 7

- This is part of a letter you received from an English friend, Peter.

> My uncle has given me some money. I want to spend it on buying computer games. My parents say I should save the money. What do you think?

- Now write a **letter** to Peter, answering his question.

Question 8

- Your English teacher has asked you to write a story.
- This is the title for your story:

An amazing conversation

- Now write your **story**.

Questions 1–7

There are seven questions in this part.
For each question there are three pictures and a short recording.
Choose the correct picture and put a tick (✓) in the box below it.

Example: Which are Sara's cousins?

  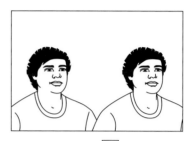

A ✓   B ☐   C ☐

---

1 Which is the family's holiday house?

A ☐   B ☐   C ☐

2 What sport has recently become available at the sports centre?

  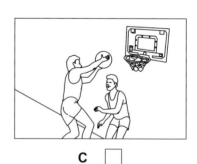

A ☐   B ☐   C ☐

3 Where is the man's wallet?

 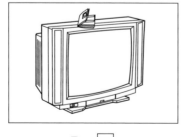 

A ☐   B ☐   C ☐

4   When did David's aunt leave?

A ☐   B ☐   C ☐

5   Which photo are they talking about?

      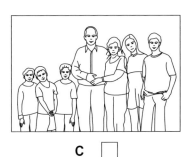

A ☐   B ☐   C ☐

6   What will the woman take on the train journey?

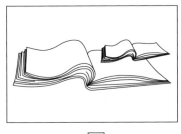   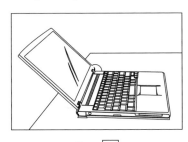   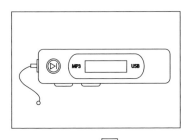

A ☐   B ☐   C ☐

7   How much will the boy pay for a ticket for the football match?

   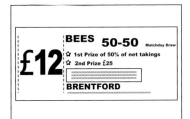   

A ☐   B ☐   C ☐

Part 2

Questions 8–13

You will hear a woman called Tina making a radio report about her recent trip to Africa.
For each question, put a tick (✓) in the correct box.

---

8   What does Tina say about the weather during her trip?

   A It rained almost every day. ☐

   B It was too hot in the day. ☐

   C It was very cold at night. ☐

9   The first journey Tina made was

   A in a small plane. ☐

   B on foot. ☐

   C by a special car. ☐

10   Tina was surprised when they saw

   A a crocodile. ☐

   B a lizard. ☐

   C a hippopotamus. ☐

11   Tina liked how close they got to

   A an elephant. ☐

   B some zebras. ☐

   C different birds. ☐

12   Tina recommends visiting Zambia on safari most to

   A young people. ☐

   B couples with children. ☐

   C retired people. ☐

13   Tina says she will never forget

   A the sunsets. ☐

   B the people she saw. ☐

   C the sense of space. ☐

Questions 14–19

You will hear a man giving a talk about a sports event to raise money for charity.
For each question, fill in the missing information in the numbered space.

Mini Olympic Games

Location: Greenford Primary School

Closing date for entries: (14) _____

Aims: to raise money for medical research.

to raise money for new (15) _____ .

to encourage children in sport.

First event starts: (16) _____ .

Parents to ensure children have enough (17) _____
on the day.

Most popular event expected to be (18) _____ .

More children needed for the (19) _____ event.

Part 4

Questions 20–25

Look at the six sentences for this part.
You will hear a mother, Marina, and her son, Sam, talking about hobbies.
Decide if each sentence is correct or incorrect.
If it is correct, put a tick (✓) in the box under **A** for **YES**. If it is not correct,
put a tick (✓) in the box under **B** for **NO**.

		A YES	B NO
20	Marina thinks Sam has fewer hobbies than his friends.	☐	☐
21	Sam thinks indoor hobbies are boring.	☐	☐
22	Sam thinks he's good at playing table tennis.	☐	☐
23	Marina enjoyed cycling when she was a child.	☐	☐
24	Marina suggests Sam joins a sports club.	☐	☐
25	Sam may spend his pocket money on a new hobby.	☐	☐

PART 1 (2–3 minutes)

Phase 1

Good morning/afternoon/evening. My name is … and this is …

Now, what's your name, *(Candidate A)*?

Thank you.

And what's your name, *(Candidate B)*?

Thank you.

(Candidate B), what's your surname? How do you spell it?

And *(Candidate A)*, what's your surname? How do you spell it?

Ask both candidates the following questions. Ask Candidate A first.
- Where do you live/come from?

Adult students
- Do you work or are you a student in …?
- What do you do/study?

School-age students
- Do you study English at school?
- Do you like it?

Thank you.

Phase 2

Select one or more questions from the list to ask each candidate. Ask Candidate B first.
- Do you enjoy studying English? Why (not)?
- Do you think that English will be useful for you in the future?
- What did you do yesterday evening/last weekend?
- What do you enjoy doing in your free time?

Thank you.

I'm going to describe a situation to you.

Your school has got some money to buy more equipment to help the students. Talk together about the different things that the school could buy and decide which ones would be the most useful for students.

Here is a picture with some ideas to help you. [*Turn to the picture on page 52.*]

I'll say that again.

Your school has got some money to buy more equipment to help the students. Talk together about the different things that the school could buy and decide which ones would be the most useful for students.

All right? Talk together.

PART 3 (3 minutes)

Now I'd like each of you to talk on your own about something. I'm going to give each of you a photograph of people taking or looking at photographs.

Candidate A, here is your photograph. [*Look at the photograph on page 53.*] Please show it to Candidate B, but I'd like you to talk about it. Candidate B, you just listen. I'll give you your photograph to talk about in a moment.

Candidate A, please tell us what you can see in the photograph.
(approximately 1 minute)

Thank you.

Now, Candidate B, here is your photograph. [*Look at the photograph on page 54.*] It shows people looking at photographs. Please show it to Candidate A and tell us what you can see in the photograph.
(approximately 1 minute)

Thank you.

PART 4 (3 minutes)

Your photographs showed people taking and looking at photographs. Now I'd like you to talk together about the things people take photographs of and the photographs people look at.

Thank you. That is the end of the test.

English Language Club
10th Anniversary

Test 1: Part 2

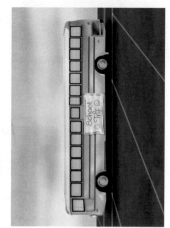

Speaking and Writing Banks

Part 1: General conversation

In this part of the test, the examiner will ask you a few questions about you and your life. Be prepared to give suitable answers on topics such as your home, your daily routine, your work, likes and dislikes, etc.

Useful language

Introducing yourself

My name's/I'm Andre Simonoviescz.

My friends call me Andy.

Giving information about yourself

I come from a (small/large) family.

I'm an only child.

I've got (an older brother) and (two younger sisters).

I live with (my parents).

My home's in (the city centre/a suburb/a small village).

I live and work in (London).

I'm studying (geography).

I'm training to be a (train driver).

I'm a (student).

I get up (quite early) every morning.

I go out with (my friends at the weekend).

I don't have a lot of spare time, but when I can, I like to (go to the cinema).

In my spare time, I (do a lot of sport).

My hobby is (gardening).

It depends on …

When you don't understand

Could you repeat that, please?

Could you say that again, please?

Please could you explain what we have to do?

I don't understand what you want me to do.

Sorry, I didn't understand that.

Exam help

- You know the answers to these questions, so reply confidently and add interesting information.

- Avoid making basic mistakes with grammar. Think about the verb tense you are going to use: is the question about the past, the present or the future?

- Activate the vocabulary area of the question. For example, if the question is about your family, think of words for family members (brother, grandmother, nephew, aunt, etc.) and for the jobs they do (teacher, shop assistant, architect, etc.).

- Speak clearly so that your partner and the two examiners can understand everything you say.

Part 2: Discussing a situation

In this part of the test, you will have to discuss a situation, based on pictures, with your partner. Be ready to share ideas and opinions.

Useful language

Asking for and making suggestions

Which (activity) do you think would be best?

What about (going swimming in the river)?

We could try (climbing trees).

I think (mountain biking) would be a good idea.

What do you think we should do?

Let's choose (the horse-riding).

Why don't we choose (the diving)?

Giving and explaining opinions

I think (a book) is best because it's (interesting).

In my opinion, (a plant) is a good idea. It (will last a long time and look pretty).

I think we should (buy her a watch) because (she hasn't got one and she's always late).

Asking for opinions

What about you?

What do you think?

Do you think (swimming) would be a good idea?

Do you agree?

Agreeing

I really agree with you.

OK, let's choose that one.

That's a good idea.

That sounds right.

That's true/right.

That's a good point.

Of course.

Definitely!

That's probably right/true.

I suppose/guess so.

Disagreeing

Maybe that's not such a great idea.

I don't know if that's the best idea.

I don't think so.

Definitely not!

I can't agree with that.

Perhaps you're right, but …

In my opinion, that isn't true.

I see what you mean, but I think …

Accepting that you have different opinions

Let's agree to disagree.

I don't suppose we'll ever agree about this.

Exam help

- Focus on the task you have been given, which requires you to discuss the options and then come to a decision together.

- Don't come to a decision too soon because you may then struggle to find other things to say.

- When your partner gives an opinion on a picture, respond fully before moving to something else. It does not matter if you do not discuss all the prompts, what is important is that you produce sufficient language at the right level.

- If your partner seems happy to let you do the talking, do involve him/her by asking his/her opinions. You will be given credit for doing that.

Part 3: Describing a photo

In this part of the test, you will talk about a photograph. You need to be able to describe different aspects of the photograph.

Describing the position of things in a photograph

in the background/
at the back

in the foreground/
at the front

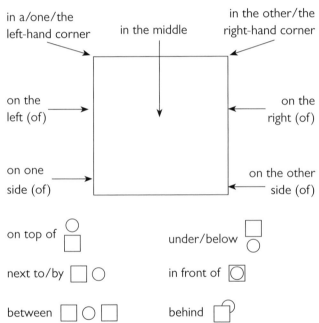

in a/one/the
left-hand corner

in the middle

in the other/the
right-hand corner

on the
left (of)

on the
right (of)

on one
side (of)

on the other
side (of)

on top of

under/below

next to/by

in front of

between

behind

In the background, there are some trees.

In the foreground, I can see two people standing.

There's a tall man holding a horse.

I can see a car driving along a big road.

On the left of the photo, there's a café with seats outside.

The table is near the window.

It's quite dark inside the room.

Saying where the people are

They're standing indoors/outdoors/by a river, etc.

They're sitting on a train/bus, etc.

They're at the beach/in a swimming pool/at a party/in a big room, etc.

They seem to be in a hotel/cinema/forest, etc.

Describing people

She's (quite/rather) short/tall/thin/fat, etc.

He's got dark/fair skin/hair, etc.

She's got short/long/straight hair, etc.

He's wearing jeans and a strange hat, etc.

Describing places

The (square) looks rather crowded.

It seems to be a very (old) (bridge).

There aren't very many (people) in the (street).

The (countryside) looks very (beautiful).

It's very (sunny) at (the beach).

Making guesses

I think they look rather sad/quite happy, etc.

They seem a bit bored/tired to me, etc.

It looks as if they're having fun/problems, etc.

Something must be (funny) because (they're laughing).

I'm not sure, but I think it might be (in China), because of (the buildings).

I don't know what this is, but I guess it's a ...

I suppose they could be (friends or sisters).

He's probably a (famous person), because (everyone's looking at him).

Maybe they're (lost).

Perhaps they (don't know which way to go).

When you don't know the name of something

I don't know what this is called in English.

It's like (an apple).

You put (dirty clothes) in it.

You use it to (change TV channels).

- Describe the photo in as much detail as you can. Talk about the people, the activities and the places. Imagine you are describing it to someone who can't see it.
- Try to use varied vocabulary and organise your description logically.
- Don't worry if you don't know a word – explain what you want to say in other words.

Part 4: Discussion

In this part of the test, you will discuss a topic with your partner. Be prepared to exchange and compare opinions and experiences.

Useful language

Giving and responding to opinions

In my opinion, it's …

I think/believe that … because …

Do you agree?

What do you think?

Are you sure?

How about you?

Expressing and asking about likes and dislikes

Do you like (playing tennis)?

What do you (like/enjoy)?

I enjoy (watching TV programmes that make me laugh).

I'm not very keen on (noisy restaurants).

I'm most interested in (music from Africa).

My favourite kind of (food is seafood/music is hip hop), etc.

I'm less keen on (riding my bike in the city).

I like/don't like (watching sport) because …

I'd rather live in (the city centre) than (a small town).

I like the (beach), but I prefer (the mountains).

I suppose if I could choose, I would (live in a big house in the forest).

Making some time to think in

That's a difficult question.

Well, I suppose that …

I'm not really sure about that, but I guess …

I haven't thought about that before, but …

It's not completely clear in the photo, but perhaps …

Exam help

- It's important to interact with your partner, asking for opinions and taking turns to speak and respond to each other.

- Don't be afraid to talk about your opinions and feelings. There is no 'correct' answer to the questions and you will not be assessed on what you think. The examiner only wants you to produce some language to show off your level.

- Try to give reasons for your opinions.

- You have now warmed up and this is the last part of your test. Enjoy the interaction and the feeling that you can express your ideas with confidence!

Part 2: Short message

Example question

(see task on page 19)

Your English friend, Julie, sent you a birthday present.

Write a note to send to Julie. In your note, you should:
- thank her for the present
- explain why you like it
- describe what you did on your birthday.

Write **35–45 words**. In the exam, you write your answer **on a separate answer sheet**.

Example answer

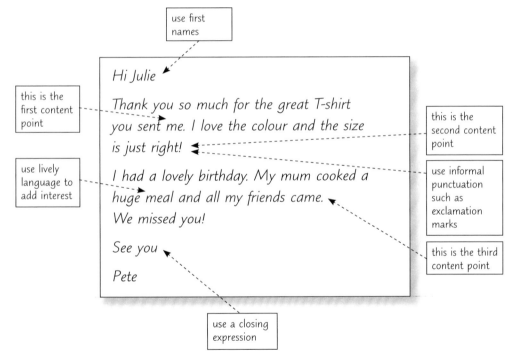

use first names

this is the first content point

use lively language to add interest

Hi Julie

Thank you so much for the great T-shirt you sent me. I love the colour and the size is just right!

I had a lovely birthday. My mum cooked a huge meal and all my friends came. We missed you!

See you

Pete

this is the second content point

use informal punctuation such as exclamation marks

this is the third content point

use a closing expression

Useful language

Thanking
I just wanted to thank you for …
Thank you so much for …
I really appreciate it.

Apologising
I'm really sorry, but …
I'm so sorry that I can't …

Suggesting and recommending
I think the best thing is to …
Why don't you … ?
Let's …

Reminding
You must remember to …
Please don't forget to …

Inviting
I hope you can …
Would you like to … ?

Explaining
I'll be late because I need to …
I like it because …

Exam help

- Read the instructions very carefully.
- Make sure you include all the content points.
- Address your email/note to the right person.
- Include a suitable closing expression.
- Check how many words you have used.
- Try to include some interesting vocabulary.
- Check your writing for mistakes.

> *Dear Julie*
>
> *Thank you for your present. I love the animals and nature. On my birthday I had to work.*
>
> *Best wishes*

Examiner's comments (Band 2)

This script is rather short (22 words). We are not sure what the present is. It is not clear whether the second content point is addressed. The language is mostly accurate. The reader would probably be a little confused by this message.

Sample answer B

> Dear Julie
>
> Thank you for remmber me and give me a nice gift I get it in my life. Really I like your present because it's remmber me for the nice day in our childhood. I so happy for the present but I too sad because you didn't come here my party.
>
> Take care

Examiner's comments (Band 3)

This script covers all three content points, although the third point is only just touched on. There are errors of spelling and some missing words, although the meaning seems to be mostly clear. The reader would basically understand the message.

Sample answer C

> Dear Julie
>
> How are you? Thank you for the present. I really like this picture because it's very beautiful and it looks very good in my home. In my birthday I went with my friends, me dancing all the night, a very funny night.
>
> See you

Examiner's comments (Band 5)

This script covers all three content points in a clear way. There are a few small errors but they do not prevent understanding. The reader would have a clear understanding of the meaning of this message.

Part 3: Informal letter

Example question

(see task on page 20)

- This is part of a letter you received from your English pen-friend.

> *I really like going to the cinema. What kinds of film do you like? Tell me about them. Why do you like them?*

- Now write a **letter** to your pen-friend about films.

Example answer

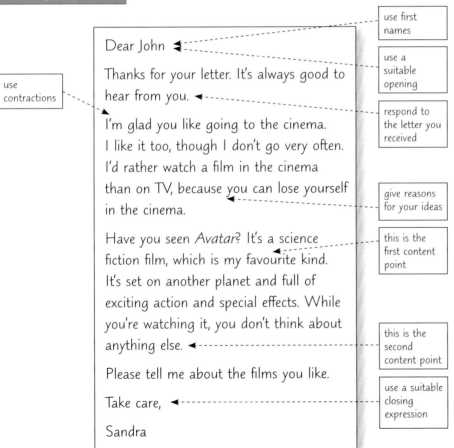

Dear John → use first names

Thanks for your letter. It's always good to hear from you. → use a suitable opening

use contractions

I'm glad you like going to the cinema. I like it too, though I don't go very often. I'd rather watch a film in the cinema than on TV, because you can lose yourself in the cinema. → respond to the letter you received / give reasons for your ideas

Have you seen *Avatar*? It's a science fiction film, which is my favourite kind. It's set on another planet and full of exciting action and special effects. While you're watching it, you don't think about anything else. → this is the first content point / this is the second content point

Please tell me about the films you like.

Take care, → use a suitable closing expression

Sandra

Useful language

Openings
Dear James
Hi James
It's always good to hear from you.
Thanks for your letter.
How are you?
I hope you're well.

Giving advice and making suggestions
If I were you …
Why don't we/you … ?
I suggest …
I think you should …
It might help to …
You could try …

Asking for and giving information
Could you tell me about … ?
I need to know …
Let me tell you about …
I thought you'd like to know about …

Giving your opinion
I agree with you that …
In my opinion, …
It seems to me that …
I believe that …
My favourite is …

Closings
Yours
Best wishes.
Write soon.
See you.
Thanks again.
Hope to hear from you soon.
Love
Take care,

Exam help

- Read the instructions very carefully.
- Address your letter to the right person.
- Write your letter in a suitable style.
- Use paragraphs to divide the letter into clear sections.
- Make sure you have included all the content points.
- Try to include interesting vocabulary to make your letter lively.
- Using linking words to join parts of your letter together.
- Count the number of words you have used.
- Try to avoid making spelling mistakes.

Sample answer A

> Dear Tina
>
> Thank you your letter. Yes, cinema is good for me too. I am going often to the cinema seeing films. All sorts films are good to watch. I like to see films that you can forget your own live for 90 minutes and joining another live. In thier live peoples they have much more bigger problems than you. I am going with my friends to the cinema so we are laughing, talking, having fun. It's great. Can you come?
>
> Best wishes

Examiner's comments (Band 2)

This isn't an adequate letter. The language is quite limited and it also contains quite a large number of basic errors, involving word order, parts of speech and expressions. It is not clear what kinds of films the writer likes, only that he or she likes going to the cinema. The question at the end is confusing. The reader has to make quite a lot of effort to read the letter, and isn't given enough information.

Sample answer B

> Dear Tim
>
> I really like going to the cinema too. I like very much adventures films. Last day I've seen for the third time Avatar because I think it's beautiful, in fact there are many special effects and the actors are very good. I love adventures films because the story is very fast, so they aren't bore me. Moreover I think it's difficult to make a film so it's neccesary to work many hours by day. I hope you write me soon again and lots of news.
>
> How is your family?
>
> Love

Examiner's comments (Band 3)

This is an adequate letter. The language is ambitious in places, although there are problems of accuracy in these places. 'seen for the third time' and 'there are many special effects and the actors are very good' are examples of successful attempts at ambitious language. On the other hand, the second sentence of the letter contains two basic errors of word order and adjective form. Phrasing such as 'they aren't bore me' require a little effort from the reader. There is a little linking language and some attempt to present the information in a sensible and logical order. The point about films being difficult to make doesn't, however, fit in very well. The reader has to make some effort to understand the letter overall.

Sample answer C

> Dear John
>
> Thank you for your letter. So you like the cinema? Me too, I like very much go to the cinema, once a month on average. I like a lots of kinds of films, and my favourite kind of film is comedy. In the second place I put the thriller and fantasy, adventure on the 3th place and at the end horror. I don't like this kind of film, in fact I hate this film. However I like comedy because when I go to the cinema I would amuse. The life is already difficult.
>
> For the other type I like thriller and fantasy for the suspense, that is very tense in some films.
>
> Write soon

Examiner's comments (Band 4)

This is a good attempt. There is some fairly ambitious use of language, such as 'once a month on average', 'very tense in some films'. There is some range of structure and vocabulary. The information is presented in a logical order, although the point about horror films doesn't really fit in. There is some linking language, such as 'however', etc. Some ambitious attempts – 'I would amuse' – that don't work completely successfully mean that a little effort is required from the reader.

Part 3: Story

Example question

(see task on page 20)

- Your English teacher has asked you to write a story.
- Your story must begin with this sentence:

  I was glad when my phone started to ring.

- Now write your **story**.

Example answer

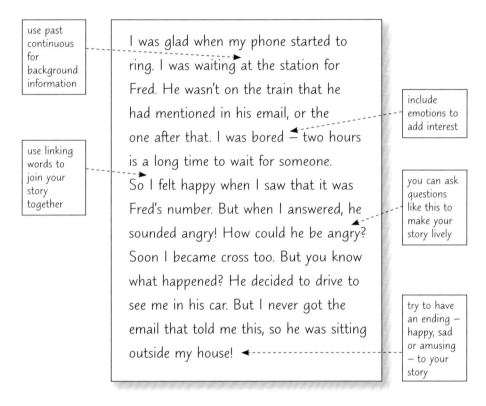

use past continuous for background information

use linking words to join your story together

I was glad when my phone started to ring. I was waiting at the station for Fred. He wasn't on the train that he had mentioned in his email, or the one after that. I was bored — two hours is a long time to wait for someone. So I felt happy when I saw that it was Fred's number. But when I answered, he sounded angry! How could he be angry? Soon I became cross too. But you know what happened? He decided to drive to see me in his car. But I never got the email that told me this, so he was sitting outside my house!

include emotions to add interest

you can ask questions like this to make your story lively

try to have an ending — happy, sad or amusing — to your story

Useful language

Adding interest
At that moment, …
Suddenly, …
Without any warning, …
Then I realised that …

Saying when things happened
It all started when …
A little later …
Meanwhile, …
Some time later, …

Using adjectives and adverbs in descriptions
It was a fantastic concert.
The dinner was absolutely delicious.
I felt completely miserable.
They both felt so scared …
It was a wonderful party.

Bringing a story to an end
It was the best day of my life.
Suddenly, I woke up.
Then I realised it was all over.

Exam help

- Read the instructions very carefully.
- If you are given a sentence to use in the story, do not change it.
- Use the names or places that you are given.
- Check your grammar, particularly verb tenses, carefully.
- Make sure you write about the right number of words.
- Use a range of vocabulary and phrases to add interest to your story.
- Divide your story into clear sections with paragraphs.

> *I was glad when my phone started to ring. I thought they bring me my new TV, but it was my frend call me and we just talking. I like my frend but I waiting TV. My frend was telling me all his day, his scool, his teacher, his frends, his families. So I was very boring. But then my phone started to ring so I was happy.*

Examiner's comments (Band 2)

This script isn't adequate. The level of language is limited – 'I waiting TV', etc. There is some attempt at a range of structure and vocabulary, but there are many very basic errors, with words missing, simple spelling mistakes and punctuation. The story is also short. Overall, the reader has to make a lot of effort to understand the story.

Sample answer B

> *I was glad when my phone started to ring. You know, I did a competition and I was waiting to the result. I answered many questions and I was surely I put right answers. But then anybody called to me so I was thinking that I lost the competition. Then I was dissaponted, becaus I wanted so much to win and then I can take my family. The price in the competition is a big holiday to safari in Africa. Then my phone started to ring. I knew it was for the competition. I knew I was the winner. I was happy really.*

Examiner's comments (Band 3)

This script is adequate. There is some ambition, although it contains mistakes at the same time – 'I was thinking that I lost the competition'. There is some range, but there are also quite basic mistakes, such as spelling mistakes, word order and missing words. There is some basic linking – 'but', 'then', etc. Overall, the reader needs to make some effort to follow the story.

Sample answer C

> *I was glad when my phone started to ring. My day had been very stressful. I was late for college, and then my teacher said my work wasn't very good, although I had tried really hard.*
>
> *I walked home but it started to rain heavily so I got soaked. By the time I got home, I was feeling really depressed.*
>
> *So you can imagine how I felt like when I realised I couldn't find my phone. Where was it? Oh no, I must lost it! But then I heard a happy noise – my phone ringing. My friend Fiona was calling me, and my phone was in my jacket after all.*

Examiner's comments (Band 5)

This script is a very good attempt. The use of language is confident and ambitious: 'it started to rain heavily so I got soaked. By the time I got home, I was feeling really depressed.' There are occasional errors, which do not make it difficult for the reader to understand, for example 'how I felt like', 'I must lost it'. Paragraphs are used to support the clear organisation of the story. Linking language helps to show this order. Overall, the reader doesn't have to make any effort to follow the story.